George Washington Carver

by Dana Meachen Rau

Content Consultant

Nanci R. Vargus, Ed.D.
Professor Emeritus, University of Indianapolis

Reading Consultant

Jeanne Clidas, Ph.D.
Reading Specialist

Children's Press®
An Imprint of Scholastic Inc.
New York Toronto London Auckland Sydney
Mexico City New Delhi Hong Kong
Danbury, Connecticut

Library of Congress Cataloging-in-Publication Data
Rau, Dana Meachen, 1971-.
  George Washington Carver/by Dana Meachen Rau.
    pages cm. — (Rookie biographies)
  Includes index.
  ISBN 978-0-531-21061-1 (library binding) — ISBN 978-0-531-24982-6 (pbk.)
1. Carver, George Washington, 1864?-1943—Juvenile literature. 2. Agriculturists—
United States—Biography—Juvenile literature. 3. African American agriculturists—
Biography—Juvenile literature. I. Title.

 S417.C3R38 2014
 630.92—dc23 [B]   2013034807

Produced by Spooky Cheetah Press
Poem by Jodie Shepherd
Design by Keith Plechaty

© 2014 by Scholastic Inc.

All rights reserved. Published in 2014 by Children's Press, an imprint of Scholastic Inc.

Printed in China 62

SCHOLASTIC, CHILDREN'S PRESS, ROOKIE BIOGRAPHIES®, and associated logos
are trademarks and/or registered trademarks of Scholastic Inc.

1 2 3 4 5 6 7 8 9 10 R 23 22 21 20 19 18 17 16 15 14

Photographs © 2014: AP Images: cover, 20, 30 right; Everett Collection: 28, 31
bottom; Getty Images/Stock Montage: 4, 30 left; National Park Service/George
Washington Carver National Monument: 15; Science Source: 27; Shutterstock, Inc./
Hong Vo: 3 bottom; Superstock, Inc.: 8, 31 center bottom (Exactostock), 11; The
Granger Collection: 3 top, 24, 31 top (Frances Benjamin Johnston), 19, 23; The
Image Works/Jeff Greenberg: 12; The Tuskegee University Archives, Tuskegee
University: 16; Thinkstock/iStockphoto: 31 center top.

Maps by XNR Productions, Inc.

Table of Contents

Meet George Washington Carver

George Washington Carver was a **trailblazer**. When he was growing up, African American people faced unfair treatment. George did not let that stop him from becoming a famous scientist and helping poor farmers.

George's love of nature led him to become a scientist.

George was born in Missouri around 1864. His mother, Mary, was a **slave** owned by Mr. and Mrs. Carver. That made George a slave, too. A slave is a person owned by someone else. Slaves were forced to work for no pay.

George was born in Diamond, Missouri.

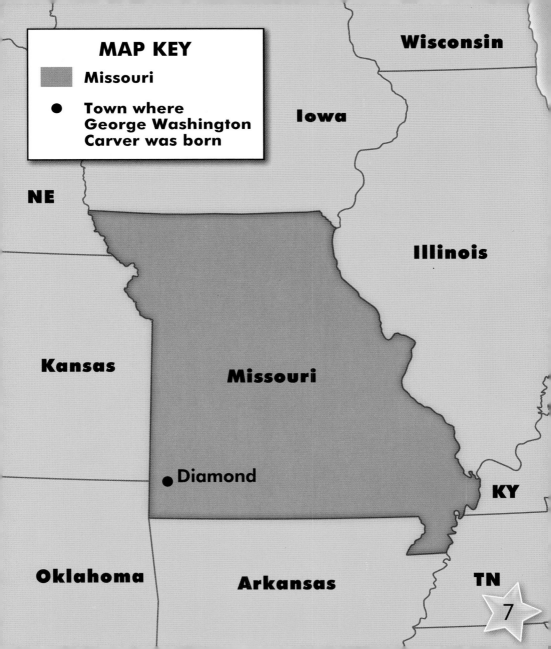

MAP KEY

▨ Missouri

● Town where George Washington Carver was born

Wisconsin

Iowa

NE

Illinois

Kansas

Missouri

●Diamond

KY

Oklahoma

Arkansas

TN

7

Many Southern farmers owned black people as slaves. When George was only a tiny baby, thieves kidnapped him and his mother. Mr. Carver traded a horse to get George back. George's mother was never seen again.

Slaves worked in the fields all day for no pay.

The Southern army surrendered to the North to end the Civil War.

The Civil War ended when George was just a baby. Now he and his brother Jim were free. Mr. and Mrs. Carver raised them as their sons. George was sickly and could not help with heavy chores. So he helped Mrs. Carver wash laundry and tend the gardens.

FAST FACT!

When neighbors needed help growing their plants, they called on young George. They called him "the Plant Doctor."

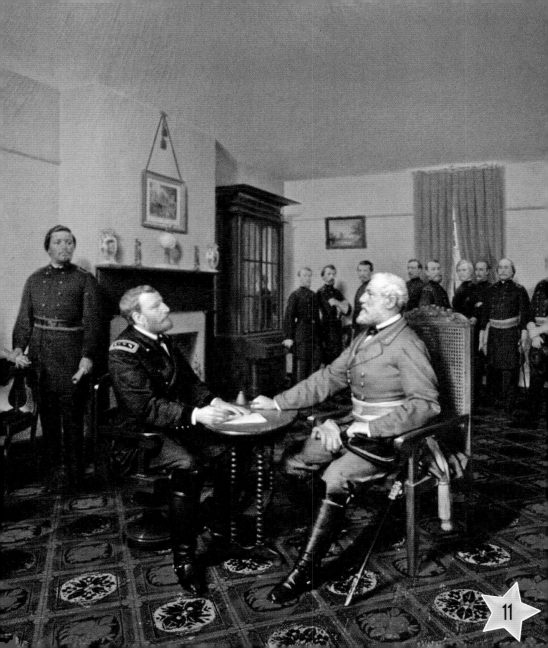

This photo shows a reproduction of the house George grew up in.

A Lifetime of Learning

George loved to paint. He also enjoyed being outdoors studying plants and collecting rocks. Mrs. Carver taught George how to read and write. He wanted to learn more, but he was not allowed to go to the nearby school because he was African American.

When George was about 12 years old, he heard about a school for black children. It was eight miles away. He left his family and walked to the distant town.

Mr. and Mrs. Watkins let George stay with them. Mrs. Watkins taught George how to use plants for medicine.

This photo of George was taken when he was 13 years old.

After finishing school, George worked at different jobs. Then he was accepted to a college in Kansas. When George went to meet the president of the college, however, he was turned away. The college would not accept black students. George moved to Iowa and entered art school.

George loved to paint pictures of flowers.

George was an excellent painter. His teacher knew it would be hard for a black man to get a job as an artist. So she urged George to study **agriculture**—the science of farming. He was the first African American student to study at Iowa State College. He even became a teacher there.

This is a photo of Iowa State College.

Professor Carver

People heard about George's work. In 1896, he was invited to be a teacher at the Tuskegee Institute in Alabama. Tuskegee was a school for black men and women. George would be the head of the school's agricultural department. He looked forward to helping poor farmers in the South.

This photo shows George at work in his lab.

Southern farmers grew lots of cotton. Planting cotton year after year was not good for the soil. It took out a lot of the **nutrients** that help plants grow. George discovered that planting different crops each year made the soil healthy again.

George taught his students how to keep farmland healthy.

George
Washington
Carver

George did not just teach the students at Tuskegee. Sometimes he brought the school right to the farmers! He taught farmers which plants were better for the soil. The peanut plant was one example. Peanuts added nutrients to the soil *and* provided food for a family.

George showed farmers the best plants to grow.

George also showed people that peanuts, sweet potatoes, soybeans, and pecans were not just for eating. He invented ways to make them into candy, oils, soap, and lots of other useful items.

FAST FACT!

George discovered how to make almost 300 products from peanuts, including cereal, milk, flour, dye, soap, candy, medicine, glue, paint, and gasoline. He also created more than 150 uses for the sweet potato.

Timeline of George Washington Carver's Life

1890
enters Simpson College to study art

around 1864
born (exact date not known)

When George died in 1943, the world lost a great scientist and a great man. Throughout his life, George had shown others the importance of treating all people fairly, no matter what their color. He cared for nature—and he cared for people, too.

1891
enters Iowa State College to study farming

1943
dies on January 5

1896
starts teaching at the Tuskegee Institute

29

A Poem About George Washington Carver

From slave, to scientist, to teacher of farmers,

a hardworking man was George Washington Carver.

With potatoes and peanuts, he was quite the magician.

He was smart and hardworking, with lots of ambition.

You Can Be a Trailblazer

- Be unique. Find your own talents and discover hobbies you enjoy.

- Ask yourself questions such as "Why?" and "How?" Then seek the answers.

- Think of how you can help others in a way that has never been done before. How can you be the "first" at something new?

Glossary

agriculture (AG-ruh-kul-chur): farming

nutrients (NOO-tree-uhnts): substances that give plants the food and minerals they need to grow

slave (SLAYV): someone who is owned by another person and thought of as property

trailblazer (TRAYL-bayz-er): a person who has new ideas or who does new things that have not been done before

31

Index

Facts for Now

Visit this Scholastic Web site for more information on George Washington Carver:

www.factsfornow.scholastic.com

Enter the keywords **George Washington Carver**

About the Author

Dana Meachen Rau has written more than 325 books for children, including lots of nonfiction and early readers. She tends her gardens with her husband and children in Burlington, Connecticut.